LOVE; Word to Live BY

<u>LOVE; Word to Live By</u>

Keith McDougall

Lulu.com

Keith McDougall
2016

First Printing: 2016

ISBN 978-1-329-99598-7

Keith McDougall
4 212 Hartley St.
Quesnel, British Columbia, Canada

V2J 1V9

stuccoman67@yahoo.ca

Dedication

I want to thank Anita Moorjani.
For sharing her beautiful story and confirming my beliefs in an afterlife.
Thanks to the publisher that told me about Lulu.com
Thanks to Lulu.com

Contents

LOVE; Word to Live By

Keith McDougall

Lulu.com

Keith McDougall
2016

Acknowledgements

I want to thank my parents for the LOVE they have always shown me, even when they don't agree with me.

I LOVE you.

THANKS.

Thanks to all of you.

Preface

On March 5, 2016 I had some kind of an awakening.
I started writing down some thoughts on politics.
On March 9, 2016 I started writing this book.
I wrote straight from my heart and experiences.
No lies.
My beliefs in god and life.
This is the first book I have written.
I hope you all enjoy.

I have started what I think is going to be a great series.
I am calling it "2110" a beautiful life.
It is going to start in 2110, and go for who knows how long.
I am already at 2122, in the first book.
I have the whole story line figured out now.
I just got to get it to paper.
My story covers Kogiee's life from birth.
To at least when Kogiee is well into his thirties.
The rest of Kogiee's family is his mother, Ana-Lucqe.
His father, Joushawalk, and sister, Skybeauty.
I hope you all like it. How can you not?
It is a perfect world coming April 4, 2016.

Introduction

I started writing this book normally.
With normal paragraphs.
I have decided to write my book in my own style.
I am hoping it is easier to read.
I think it is easier to find your spot on the page.
I think I made words on a page look pretty.
I know weird.

This is the 17th time I have revised this book.
The number 17 means a lot to me.
On august 17th 1949 my mom was born.
I LOVE her very much.
On January 17th 1976 (BEAUTIFUL) was born.
I LOVE her very much.
On September 17th 1999 (BEAUTIFUL) died in a work accident.
You will read about (BEAUTIFUL) in my story.

It has now been 17 years since her accidental death.
All those 17 teens in my life is the reason.
I will never change this book again.
I hope I did well and you all enjoy it.

So I hope I fixed all my mistakes.
I know I do not have all the comas in the right places.
I am sorry for that I did try my best I am learning.

This is a book I truly wrote from my heart about my life and my many thoughts about life.
I am not trying to force my views on anybody.
My goal is for a happier life for us all.
I believe there are lots of people out there that think like me.
I just want them to know they are not alone.
None of us are.

I hope everyone can take something positive from my stories.
I do know not everyone is going to agree with every chapter.
I am hoping at least one-chapter will relate to you.
I tried my best.
If you want to discuss your points of view.
Go to.
E-mail   stuccoman67@yahoo.ca

You can teach me something.
I am more than willing to learn.
I am 48 years Old.
I know I have lots to learn.
This is my first book.
I am rather proud of it.
I hope you enjoy.

<u>Chapter 1: In the beginning</u>

I do not know if GOD is real but I do believe.
I believe in the beginning GOD gave us all we need.
All we will ever need.
GOD made us perfect.
GOD gave us the best gift of all.
The truly amazing and beautiful gift we call life.

With all the love GOD has for us and all the creations of Earth.
GOD gave us someone or something to love.
GOD provided us with fruit, vegetation, water and the want to survive.

I think our little planet works too perfectly not to have a creator of some sort.
When you look out in the sky and see all those other planets.
They all look dead.

I feel like we are special and very lucky to have the gift of life.

I believe that there is a GOD.
Our planet works too perfectly to provide us with all we need.
Every spring brings new life and hope for the future.
New fruit, vegetation and water.

If there is no GOD who provided us with all the fruit trees?
The vegetation that grows every spring.
The fresh water that flows from the mountains.
I am guessing we had all this stuff before we even knew we needed it.
I would imagine that the first people damn near starved before they found out that they could eat the fruit from the trees.
Of course there is a GOD.

I believe LOVE, PEACE, and HARMONY are the keys to life.
To truly know LOVE we would love all creatures.
Everything that thinks has to Love and is alive.

What gives any of us the right to decide what lives or dies?
If we truly knew LOVE we would not kill.

I do not think we were meant to kill.
We should not kill anything that thinks.
If it thinks then it feels.
If it feels then it must LOVE.

Just because we can take life does not mean we should.
There are lots and lots of things we do that we should not do.
We think we need to kill to protect ourselves and our families.
If we truly LOVED we would not want to kill.
You would LOVE that person or animal.
You would not want to kill them.

All the animals naturally stay away from us.
Even the biggest of animals stay away.
They are so big and strong.
They could kill us easily and do not.
Even the animals are smart enough to know we have to live in
PEACE and HARMONY with each other.

I believe when the planet and everything on the planet starts to
work together to create life.
Rather than destroying life.
This is when we would get to experience the true beauty of life.

I would think GOD is really not happy with us.
We kill on a mass scale.
By this I mean wars and farms.
The wars kill humans and many other living, breathing and
thinking creatures.
Wars fought for countries wanting to profit.

Instead of killing one another.

Why not have x-games military style or put your best fighter in the ring.

We have the abilities and brains to come up with solutions.
The solutions to solve our problems without killing.

The farms are killing many of GODS creatures.
Killing for the convenience of laziness and Fast food.
Fast food and processed foods are killing us.

No wonder so many of us do not feel right and cannot seem to find happiness.
Did you know?

Sugar is eight times more addictive than cocaine.
Sugar should be outlawed.
Another example of the lies the government tells us.

Watch "fed up" the movie.
It will blow your mind about the food industry.
This documentary enforces my thoughts and views on the food industry.
Decide for yourself.

We must know deep inside of us that we are not living properly.

What gives any of us the right to take life?
Do we think we are better or smarter than what we are killing?
Just because it is an animal we think it does not matter.

I know if I was GOD and someone killed one of my creations.
A creation that I loved enough to create.
I would not be happy.
So in saying that.
I cannot see how GOD approves of the way we live.
Can you?

I believe all the diseases and cancers that exist in the world today is a direct result of the way we are living and from what we are eating.

If we eat the fruits of life and lived off of mother nature.

We would live a healthier life and maybe a happier life a more meaningful life.

GOD provided us with all the fruits and vegetation we need to survive.

In my way of thinking it only stands to reason.

GOD is perfect.

GOD created the perfect environment for us to live in.

GOD must have made all the cures we need as well.

I think if we get back to a natural way of living.

There would be less and less disease.

I believe GOD has put a cure for any disease in a plant, a fruit or maybe a source of milk.

I cannot see how GOD got all the fruit and vegetation right.

GOD must have gotten all the cures right as well.

I believe if there is a GOD.

GOD would not be jealous or vain.

That is why in my thoughts I think religion is all wrong.

Religion has started more wars in the name of GOD and country.

All the way back to the beginning of religion.

One of their religious quotes,

"Thou shall not harm thee neighbor."

Well unless thee neighbor does not believe in my GOD.

Then it is alright to kill.

Not likely.

I really think these guys that follow a religion that tells them it is ok to sin.
All you have to do is confess your sins.
What a joke.

Who are you confessing your sins to?
If there is a GOD.
GOD is seeing everything you have done.
GOD is not going to believe your lies.
I am sorry but way to convenient.
If there is a GOD.
GOD must just be shaking his head in disgust.
What use or need would a GOD have for our treasures?

If there is a GOD.
All GOD would want for us.
Is to LOVE.
The same way GOD LOVES us by providing all we need.

I am not putting down all religion.
There are religions that if you truly believe.
You will not commit any sins.
You are only going to be a kind and decent human being.
What is wrong with that?

It is the people that claim to be religious and then they commit sins.
Sins like Murder, Theft and Rape.
Then they think they can get away with it.
All they have to do is repent and all is forgiven.

I guess that is between them and GOD.
Just some thoughts that I have what do I know.

The temptations of life have sent us spiraling down the wrong path.
How dumb are we?
Do we think killing for oil rights or for any reason is alright with GOD?

I imagine a GOD that would hope we never found a use for oil.
Do we actually think that when GOD created earth?
GOD thought to himself,
"Self I am thinking in a few thousand years my loving people are going to need oil."

I do not believe we need to drill for oil.
There are other ways of producing oil and fuel.
Ways that do not take drilling.
Check into it if you do not already know.

The discovery of oil was the beginning of mass laziness.
With all the conveniences that oil brought to us.
Oil probably does have a purpose.
That is why GOD hides it deep down inside the earth.

GOD was probably thinking,
"My LOVING people will not be stupid enough to dig that deep into their planet."
"I hope they do not find oil this time and destroy this planet like they did to the last one."
Just my thoughts.

Here is a poem.
Well my attempt at a poem.

I call it "GOD is PISSED."

Is there a GOD?
I do not know but I do believe.
If there is a GOD.
Do we think we are making him happy by killing?
Killing other living, breathing, thinking creations.

GOD is PISSED.

Do we think GOD wants us to kill?
In his name religion or for our country?

GOD is PISSED.

Do we think GOD is ok with us killing any of his creations?
A living, breathing, thinking creature just because it is different than us.

GOD is PISSED.

Why would GOD give us the power to be able to settle our problems without KILLING?

GOD is PISSED.

GOD gave us all we need.
LOVE and the LOVE for the opposite sex.
GOD gave us the want for PROCREATION.
I LOVE it.
Such a smart GOD.
GOD gave us fruit, vegetation, water and the want for survival.
GOD did not give us M16s and the weapons of mass destruction.
Weapons that kill from miles away so far away they do not even have to see what and how many of GODS creations they are killing.

GOD is PISSED.

We have to start LOVING all GODS creations.

LOVE, PEACE and HARMONY I think that was GODS plan. DEFIANTLY not war.

GOD is PISSED.

I like my poem.
What do you think of it?

I believe the only constant in our lives.
From the beginning of time is LOVE.

I am not talking sex.

We LOVE and we hurt when we lose LOVE or when LOVE is taken from us.

I think LOVE is what we live for.

LOVE has to be the key to a happy life.

I think GOD LOVES us so much.

GOD would never want to see us truly die.

I do believe in heaven and reincarnation.

I am having some new thoughts on reincarnation.

I am thinking this life is full of learning.
Right from birth we start learning.
Till the day we die.

I think we take what we learn from here to our next lives.

I believe our last life is what gives us that feeling inside of right and wrong.

I am guessing that if we kill and take life.
This would be GODS only crime.

The punishment for such a crime is to be reborn a chance to get life right.

When I was 18 years old I tried to take my own life my heart was broken.

I had cheated on my girlfriend and naturally she dumped me.

I was crushed.

I remember thinking I have had enough of this life.

I wanted to start over.
It seemed so clear to me.
So I ate a bunch of pills.

I never wrote a note or anything like that all I was thinking about was myself and the idea of starting over.
It was not very long after I took the pills.
When the phone rings it was my girlfriend.

She wanted me to come over where she was babysitting.

I was so happy I forgot about taking the pills.

I am not too sure how long I was there for before I started to pass out.
It did not take her long to figure out there was something wrong with me.

She called her parents and they took me to the hospital.
When I woke up the next day in the hospital all I was thinking about was my girlfriend.
Not what I had done.

I have never ever had thoughts of suicide since.
Even though I have been through some extremely harsh times.

I have not looked to suicide for the easy way out since then.

I am thinking the act of taking one's own life is still killing.

We will have to answer to GOD for such a crime.
Why would such a perfect GOD want us in Heaven?
Especially if we do not know how to live in PEACE and HARMONY with others.

I think If death really is the end.
Nothing in this life would make any sense.
Why learn or do anything.
Deep down in all of us I think we know this is not the end.

I think the only reason we have butterflies and goldfish.
Is to show us the magic they have.

Butterflies are so beautiful.

They start their first life as a slow moving creature that cannot even jump.

In their second life.

They are beautiful creatures that can glide through the air.

Goldfish have the ability to freeze and thaw then come back to life.

Why can these creatures perform this kind of magic and we have no powers at all.

I think rebirth is the reason some people are good at what they do.

Like excel at sports, music or anything they are good at.

I believe this is what we call evolution.

Deep in us we remember from our last life and it makes us better in this life.

I think that is why babies have nightmares.

They are remembering their last life.

I believe that is why some baby's cry a lot.

I am thinking they died an unnatural way.

They are remembering their last life or life's.

I believe the baby's that do not cry so much from dreaming.

Died a more natural way they have a more peaceful transition to this live.

If I am wrong and this is the baby's first time living.

What would a baby dream about?

Why would they have nightmares?

They have not yet lived through or seen anything scary.

What are the dreams from?

I have the same questions for a blind person.

If they were blind from birth.

When they dream if they have never seen before.

What do they dream about what do they see?

If they do have vision in their dreams that would prove they must have lived before and had vision.

I believe I was probably killed in a war my last life.

When I was young I remember being scared of the idea of war.

Being scared of turning 19 and getting drafted and having to go to war.

Yes I was that young and dumb to think we still had the draft. Maybe that was just a memory?
The older I got and the farther away from that life I got.
The fear eventually went away.
When I turned 19 I actually went and signed up for the army.
I never did go through with it.

I do believe in KARMA.
What I have learned about Karma is that the acts of kindness we are rewarded for is not in this life.
The acts of kindness in this life are rewarded in our next life as KARMA.
This to me makes way more sense.
A perfect GOD would give us little encouragements and rewards for living a kind life.

I think we have to stop the killing and start being kind to each other and stop being jealous of what your neighbor has.
We have to start being happy with what we have LIFE.
I have no need to be better than anybody my needs are simple.
I need air I want LOVE in my life.
SIMPLE.
Of course there is a GOD.

If there is no GOD and we choose to try and live by these words. What could happen?
We start to LOVE each other and start to help each other.
I am thinking it is a fuller and more rewarding way to live.
We might get to see the true beauty in life.
It is everywhere.
Of course there is a GOD.

RANDOM THOUGHTS

Now that we can communicate with the whole world through the internet.

We should be able to do study's that would look at the time of birth or when they say the baby has thought.
Maybe when their sex develops.

Then you try to find out if there was a death near that time.

I am guessing there will be.
Then you find out all the information on the deceased pictures, video and handwriting.
All the info that is possible.

Keep track of the baby and family with their permission of course.
When the baby is old enough start comparing to what info you have.

I am guessing the younger the better.
Looking for habits things they excel at.
If you have pics be looking for eye color hair color stuff like that.
It would be nice to prove there is an after LIFE.

I wonder if there is someone somewhere already doing these studies.
It is in our DNA to want to know for sure about life after death.

I will see if I can find anything like that online.

I went online.
Holy there is lots of study's happening on the subject.
There is proof.

People that have had an N.D.E.

(near death experience)
When they come back to their bodies.

They claim to have seen things happening miles away.
So they now go to where they claim to have seen these things happening.
Guess what.

The events they saw in there N.D.E. happened they did see it.

Even if it happened miles away thousands of miles away.

The one thing they all have in common when they come back to their life is they lose the fear of death and enjoy their life's more. Of course there is a GOD.

Chapter Two: War

Since the beginning of time we have been fighting wars.
Wars caused by religion and or greed.
The greed for money or power.
Wars fought for men that are sitting at home with their
families and loved ones.
With no real knowledge of the impact on the family's they are killing
on both sides of the senseless conflict.
They make weapons bigger and bigger so they can kill and take
larger amounts of life with one devastating blow.

In my way of thinking this is the evilest thing I could imagine.
Why do we think it is alright to kill because of a difference in opinion
greed or any reason really?
Who has the right to keep anyone from their LOVED one?

On both sides of any war has people that are killing each other.
Taking someone's dad, mother, and sibling or loved one away.

I watched a show on war veterans.
These guys went and killed for their country.
When they come home a lot of them are depressed.
They have brutal images in their thoughts.
Thoughts of the evil they have seen all the death, murder and so on.
They call this P.T.S.D.
Twenty-two U.S. veterans commit suicide every day.
That is just wrong it is a huge number.
The governments answer to help them.
Is to give them all these pills to help the P.T.S.D.
It is not working HELLO!!!!! WAKE UP!!!!!

This kind of stress has happened since the beginning of time.
Any war has caused P.T.S.D.
Instead of trying to find a cure.
I know the cure.

Stop the KILLING it is unnatural and evil.

All of the GODS living, breathing, thinking creations bleed red.
All of us.

I think this is a definite sign of a GOD.
In how much we are all alike.

We all need LOVE and air to live.

The color red that flows through all of us is the same red.
Why is blood red why not blue or green?
Maybe to warn us.
If we see red flowing we know that it must be blood.

Blue is seen everywhere in the skies and all the water.

Green is all over the ground and in the forests.

The color red is not seen every day.

We only see red in mans creations.

We as GODS creations are that unique and special.
Of course there is a GOD.

I think war is brutal.

I am not going to waste any more thoughts on it.
War is such a waste of life.

Of course GOD is PISSED.

RANDOM THOUGHTS

I believe politics is the main cause of our demise.
We all know they lie.
They make false promises and we just accept it.
Are we all on glue?
Why would we ever let this happen?

I have never voted and probably never will.
I do not support them at all.
If we really do want to improve our life's and environment.
We have to make a change.

We do not alloy one man/women to run the country.
It is too easy to force one person into evil decisions.
Every political group should have one leader we the people vote for.
A true voice for the people.

No more time and money that is wasted on campaign trails.
Instead they can actually be doing their jobs.

We have pretty good technologies with lie detectors now a day.
We take the leaders of each party and hook them up to a lie
detector when they step up to the podium one after another.
We ask them questions on their future plans for us.
The first and most important question they are asked,
"Is your plan to improve the lives of every living, breathing, thinking
creation in your control?"
If the answer is no or the lie detector goes off.
Do not vote for that person.

The world would be the exact opposite.
You vote for your politician knowing they are telling the truth.

I just do not get how we ever let our world get run on lies.
I believe if we started to LOVE ourselves enough to want the
truth and run our lives with truth instead of lies.
We would have better home lives.
Our relationships would benefit totally from truth instead of the lies.

Living in a consent world of lies has to be ruining our lives right to our SOULs.
How can we truly LOVE ourselves if we do not take a stand and stop listening to the lies?
Let us wake up and make sure there will be a future.
Stop the lies and we can stop evil.

Taxes would be kept in country.
Why would we work to pay taxes that are supposed to improve or at least maintain our life styles?
Medical, education, roads and so on.
Why would we send our taxes to a different country?
If we want to send our hard earned money to a charity or country.
That is up to us.
No way should our leaders have the power to just spend our tax money.
The spending of our tax money should be voted on by the people.

When we let people that we know are lying to us run the WORLD.
We deserve everything we get.
We get screwed and not in a gentle way.
Just Evil.
I really do not get it I know we cannot all be this stupid to believe the lies we are told on a daily basis.

Chapter Three: Death

I believe in reincarnation as I have said before.
When I was young I had a beautiful childhood.
Up till I was 12 years old.
I will get into that later on for now back to my innocence.

I played and enjoyed my youth.
I never wasted any time on homework it just was not for me.

My parents were the best I felt a lot of love from them.
Even with all the love I never felt quite right.
I always had thoughts about death.
Why we are here.
What does it all mean and what happens after death.
For as far back as I can remember whenever I do not have something to do or a way to keep my mind occupied.
I would have these thoughts.
Sometimes I cannot stop thinking about this kind of stuff.
At those times I cannot sleep and find it hard to relax.
Pacing and thinking.
I guess maybe that is why we drink alcohol or do drugs.
To stop our thoughts or at least slow them down.

I use to be scared of DEATH.
I remember being in between eight and I would guess eleven.
Somewhere in there.
I can remember being scared of dying.
As I thought about dying I decided death was nothing to fear.
Death happens to everybody nobody gets out alive.

I had a calming feeling come over me and eventually came to believe in reincarnation.
I believe we are all too big and powerful for this to be all there is to our being.
I told myself that,
"There was no way this LIFE could be all there is for us being."
I have not been scared of death since.

That might be why when I tried to comment suicide I was not scared.

If it was not for "Heart Break 3" calling me to come over I would probably be dead.

I would have gently gone to sleep and there is a really good chance that I might not have woken up in my body.

That did not happen so who really knows. Maybe just not my time.

I do not fear death I also do not encourage it.

I have recently come to LOVE my life.

I finally get what I was meant to do.

I am Forty-Eight years old.

On the 5 of march 2016.

It was a Saturday night.

I was sitting in my room thinking about politics.

Wondering how wrong I think we are all living believing all the lies.

I thought about writing all my thoughts down.

I started writing on my cell phone.

I have since moved to a laptop using micro soft word.

As I wrote my thoughts down.

I would go back and read what I had written my words sounded right.

I thought I was making sense.

The words and ideas have just been flowing none stop.

So I was thinking I should write a newspaper column about my thoughts opinions and my views on life.

I figured there must be some people out there that can relate to what I am saying.

What would be better than giving HOPE or letting someone know that they are LOVED and are not alone in the world.

Let them know someone thinks the same way they do.

On the ninth of march 2016 I decided to write this book.

This was on a Wednesday.

I found it so easy to write my words and thoughts down.

Then on the very next day while I was writing.

I probably was just starting chapter two I had gone for a coffee and my mom was watching Dr. Oz.

Dr. Oz had Anita Moorjani on his show.

Anita is the author of "Dying to be me."

I had never heard her story before.

I thought I would see what she had to say.

Anita changed my life the best thing I have ever done was learning Anita's story.

I have now watched lots of Anita's interviews and her stand up sessions.

Anita has a beautiful story.

She lived through and beat cancer.

I am not going to tell all her story.

Only hopefully enough to enforce my thoughts and views.

I am trying to get a hold of her to ask if this is alright.

I am going to give my new thoughts.

On LIFE and Death because of her story.

RANDOM THOUGHTS

We have become a world that we allow the government to tell us what is legal or not legal.

The only laws that should be allowed is murder, rape, theft and road laws.

The government should not have the power to dictate how an individual chose to live.

They should not be able to tell us that a plant GOD created is illegal.

If we are not hurting anyone by using this plant.

Why do they have these stupid LAWS in place?

If we allow laws to be enforced just to keep the rich, rich.

We are failing as compassionate caring NATURE LOVING human beings.

Are we not smart enough to see through all the lies?

These lies have to be evil.

How can this same government that says our little plant is illegal?

Make a medicine using this same plant.

Put a bunch of crap in it and change its name then they sell it to the public for profit.

EVIL.

How can we allow a government to not help dying children?

To not give them quite possibly a cure.

All because the cure is illegal how evil is this?

We must be letting the devil run our lives.

I just cannot see how GOD would be letting this happen.

If someone especially a child dies.

All because we did not try everything known to man to save them.

We are evil the devil is winning.

Let us stand together and change our world for a better tomorrow.

The future is ours all of OURS.

Let us stop the evil together and make sure we all have a future.

Chapter Four: Anita's blessings

To my surprise seeing Anita's interview and learning about her story.

She confirmed some of what I have always known or maybe felt.

Anita explains about feeling LOVE on the other side after her Near Death Experience.

I have said I believe it is all about LOVE.
Anita would know way more than me she was there.
I have just always had these feelings on an afterlife.

Anita experienced something beautiful.
She learnt that we are all connected in the other realm.
Anita felt unconditional LOVE in the other realm.

Anita did not die she was very close but her heart never stopped beating.

So I am thinking that maybe our heart and mind is what connects us to Earth.

What locks our souls in our body.

When our heart stops we have no choice.

We have to leave this body.

I am thinking of our body's like a car when the motors gone.

You buy a new car a better car.

That makes me think of evolution.

We live longer than we did a hundred years ago.

How long will the average person live for in another hundred years.

We are also much stronger for the most part.

Anita said that when she was in the other realm.

She had the choice of staying or coming back to her cancer riddled body.

Naturally she did not want to come back.

Anita's father who had died ten years earlier.

Told her if she came back there would be gifts waiting for her.

He told Anita it was not her time.

Anita knew that meant her body would heal.
So she came back to her body.

I believe Anita's gifts were a cancer free body and the memory of her experience to share with all of us.
If you have not read her book or do not know who she is.
I recommend it.

Now I am wondering.
Anita said she had a choice to stay in the other realm or comeback.

I have a wild question.
If when we have a Near Death Experience, and have the power to come back to Earth.
What if you have been Near Death multiple times in one life.
Would we have the power to choose what time in our lives we want to come back to?
Could there be study's done on this?

What if we could learn to slow down our heart enough to cause a Near Death Experience.
Creating an entire point to that time in our life.
When we are in Heaven we would then go have a chat with our lost love ones.
Then come back to our body when we are done with our visit.
On the following year you create another N.D.I.
Then when we chose to come back to our body.
Would we be able to come back at an earlier time in our life?

I know that is way out there but to some of us.
So is the idea of an afterlife or a GOD.

I would LOVE to be the subject of an out of body experience.
I want to try it at two deferent times in my life.
In-between crossovers I would study lotto numbers.
Then create a second crossover.
If we have a choice to come back.

I would pick to come back to my first cross over.

I would think if we had entry points we could choose what time in our life's we come back to.

So by studying the lotto and choosing my second entry point in my life which is my first crossover.

My first entry point being birth.

Knowing the winning lotto numbers could prove I was the future me. If anybody reading this can cause an out of body experience.

Get a hold of me.

We could change the world.

To talk a little about time travel.

I would love to go back in time.

Not to become rich because of the knowledge I would take back with me.

That would be a bonus.

My reason would be to save a life.

I would think the key here on earth.

To be able to do such a thing like time travel would only become a reality.

If we could ride a beam of light.

Light and electricity is our answer to time travel.

If at all possible.

I know most of you think I am just talking crazy now.

Maybe I am but if you think about it.

If we could go back in time.

We would tell the people of 1850 all about TV's, cars, planes and cell phones.

They would think we lost our minds.

All these unthinkable ideas all became realty.

Anita said time was not the same in the other realm.

Everything was happening all at once.

Anita was able to comprehend everything that was happening to her.

Ok imagine looking down at Earth.

You are seeing all the life that has ever happened since the beginning of time.
And all the life happening on Earth right now.
To me that would be incomprehensible.

Anita seen past life's happening at the same time as her current life.
To me that is time standing still for her and on earth everything is happening all at once.

Anita does not mention seeing a future life.

I think if we have had past lives we are going to have a future life.
Maybe when we are crossed over and the fact that time is still happening on Earth.
Maybe all we can do is review our past life's and learn from them.
With all the beauty and magic that is the afterlife.
I guess we really can never know.

Anita said she felt unbelievably good in the other realm.
She saw more beauty and color then we have here on earth.
Sounds BEAUTIFUL to me.

I think maybe we have it all wrong.
Maybe death is a beautiful thing.
The ones that die young in life are actually the lucky and truly blessed.
I am thinking maybe we should celebrate and rejoice death just like we do with birth.
Death happens to all of us.
The only two things all us humans truly know we all do the same.
We are born and we all die.

I think death is just a part of life.
Why can't it be beautiful?
If we truly knew our LOVED ones are in a better place.
A beautiful place.
We would defiantly celebrate their good fortune.

Being human we would probably be a bit jealous of them.

If we truly LOVED.
LOVE would change a lot for us.
We would not hate for murder.
How could we hate someone for sending a loved one to a better place.
If we truly LOVED there would be no murder anyhow.

Anita's experience taught her we are all forgiven.
There is nothing but LOVE and acceptance in the afterlife.

I do not know if all is forgiven in Heaven.
I think Anita probably lived a kind and loving life even before her Near Death Experience.
Anita has to be a special person.
She went to Heaven and came back.
If everyone could do that it would happen all the time.

I wander what kind of an experience an evil soul would have.
I think there has to be some kind of punishment for harsh crimes against humanity.
Maybe that is one of my flawed ways of thinking.
Maybe all is forgiven and there is no punishment for crimes commented on Earth in heaven.
One day we are all going to find out the secrets of life and the afterlife.

I just wish I could figure it out before I die not after.
That might be the biggest joke about life.
We live trying to find out the meaning of life.
The purpose of life.
Which in turn probably wastes our LIFE?
A life where we always fear death.
When all we have to do is die.
To get the answers we seek.
Bad joke but really do you get it.

Just live and enjoy life.

LOVE life before it is over and we finally find out what life is all about.

RANDOM THOUGHTS

I am watching a show called "HUMAN."
A documentary about LOVE.
I saw the coolest story.
A Grandson is talking to his Grandpa about Grandpa's wife of
65-years dying.
The Grandson asks Grandpa,
"How are you doing Grandpa?"
Grandpa replies,
"Did you know I can catch a shuttle for only four dollars anywhere in
town."
The Grandson smiles and says,
"That is great grandpa."
Grandpa continues to tell about his day's travels.
"I went to the market with my shopping list."
I asked the lady at the counter,
"If she could help me find the items on my list"
I told the lady I needed her help because,
"My wife has recently relocated her residents to heaven."
The grandson smiles and says,
"Thanks Grandpa for showing me the glass is always half full."
Grandpa answers,
"Ya it is such a BEAUTIFUL glass."

I take the story as the GLASS being LIFE and what's in the
GLASS is LOVE.
I do not know who Grandpa is in this story but I LOVE grandpa
for sharing his story on LOVE.
To me Grandpa knows there is no need for feeling the loss of a
LOVED one.
I am sure Grandpa still feels his LOVE close to him.

The stories from this documentary show us what LOVE looks like
from all over the world.
If we LOVED and CARED the way we are capable of.
Most of these stories in this documentary would not have been told.

Chapter Five: Beautiful body

A whole lot of maybes with no real answers.
I do not really have any answers.
I do believe in Anita's beautiful story.
Now when Anita came back to her body.
Within weeks the cancer was gone.
Leaving no trace.
Anita says we have the power to heal or make our self's sick.

I have always known that.
Not sure why but I have always thought we can control our health.
Our mind is capable of way more than we allow it.

Talking about the brain.
Is our mind what gives us thought or is it our soul that gives us thought.
Maybe our brain is just the computer for our soul.
If we listen to our soul instead of what our brains have been taught since birth.
The powers we might one day have again.

I think if Anita had thought and
Comprehension when she was in the other realm.
That would prove our thoughts are produced from our souls or spirit.
So we should defiantly listen to our soul.
Our SOUL is the only thing that goes from here to there.
It is not our body's or brains.

I am thinking maybe way back when the pyramids were being built.
Maybe we were able to do what we now consider GOD like acts of strength.
Over many years with all the negative input and being taught our limitations from birth.
By being taught what to fear like death.

Being called stupid or being told that we are too ugly or too fat to find LOVE.

Those should be the true swear words.

The words our children should never hear.

All that negative input is no good for anybody.

Instead of being taught about limits and being told what we cannot do.

We should only teach our children what they can do and how BEAUTIFUL and unique they are.

When we put limits on others abilities we hold them back.

How do I know what one man's limits are from another man?

Why would I care?

The result from years of being told these limits.

We eventually lost or forgot how to tap into our true potential.

This could explain Jesus walking on water and healing people.

If GOD created us in his image.

Why would he not give us the abilities of a GOD as well.

I am not suggesting we are GODS but if any man could do such things.

We would think of him as a GOD.

Instead of telling your child,

"He/she cannot run faster than your fasted dog" for example.

Encourage him/her to train if he/she wants to be that fast.

Do not put limits on them.

You have no right or idea what their true potential is or might be.

Just show LOVE and give only positive input.

I am guessing you will have an amazing child.

I have not been to a doctor in over thirty years.

I feel just as good as I did in my twenty's.

I do not believe a doctor knows my body better than me.

After all I have been me for forty-eight years and aging.

I read a story about a lady that lived to be a hundred and twenty-five years old.

She never had a sickness other than a common cold.
She could still walk, talk and think tell the day she died.
Do you know what she used every day?
She smoked cannabis.
I thought that plant was supposed to be bad for us.
Wrong just more lies we are told.
Time to wake up.

I do not believe in the doctors of today.
For the most part I believe today's doctors did not become a doctor to save lives.
Most not all became doctors for money, power or forced by their parents.
Not like the doctors of the old days wanting to save a life or make life a little easier and better for others.

Instead of thinking about others.
We have become a world that thinks only of ourselves and what will benefit me.
The feeling I get from holding that door open or buying a coffee for the person behind me.
Is a feeling of beauty enrichment and joyful.
I am not sure if we have the proper word for this feeling.
Maybe that is the inner feeling of LOVE.
I would LOVE to have this feeling every woken moment.
So far in life I do not think there is a job.
Where I can just go and be kind to people all day long and get paid.
If there is I would like to apply.

Unfortunately in this world it takes money to live.
Something as natural as life costs money.
From the time we are born tell death.
Even after death it cost someone money.

We should not have to pay to be born.
Unreal the future of all life depends on the new born.
How can we put a cost on our futures?
Animals give life and live with no money.

We should learn from GODS smarter creatures.
We consider ourselves the smartest creation on earth.
I am thinking the animals are way ahead of us.

Why do we think GOD loves today's man more than the first man?
GOD gave us all we need.

I believe GOD would have given us all we have now.
If he wanted us to be where we are now.
A GOD that would have the power to create the Earth and everything on Earth.
Would also have the power to create a car.
After all we came up with the car.

I am sure GOD saw this path way before we did.
If GOD thought we needed it we would have it.
GOD gave us horses, camels and elephants all gentle creatures when shown LOVE.
These ride able creatures do not need gas or anything that we do not need.

Why would we ever need cars or any unnatural transportation?
To get from one place to another faster.
What is at that place?
Why do we need to get there any faster?

I think the harsh reality of this world is we all LOVE money more than LIFE.

If we went down GODS path.
Used what GOD gave us to use.
Never put limits on ourselves and our children.
GOD never gave us limits why should we?

I believe living GODS way we would not need any of our technologies.
If we used our minds and bodies in GODS vision for us.
We would have all these powers on our own.

With no man made machine.

Why is GOD the greatest creator?
It is because he made us.
GOD created us so that our bodies and minds work together as one.
No man made machine even comes close to us.
This is why I do not understand how man can think we are so much smarter than GOD.
Why do we think we need anything GOD did not already give us?

RANDOM THOUGHTS

The next chapter is about LOVE.

I am sorry if I offend anybody I did not mean to.

I hope you all enjoy my thoughts and story's.

I have enjoyed writing these pages like nothing I have felt before.

I am so excited in the hope that you are reading my thoughts.

I really hope that there are more people out there feeling the same as me.

That are feeling and thinking about what I have to say.

I am hoping the shivers I feel as I write are from the connection we all have and my words are coming from all of you.

If I am wrong about some of my thoughts.

I am sorry I am only human.

I know something's have been confirmed for me through Anita's beautiful story.

Also through these other incredibly   beautiful stories' like "HEAVEN is REAL" and "MIRACLES from HEAVEN."

I believe we are allowed to hear these BEAUTIFUL stories to give us hope.

To let us know this is not the end.

I do not think these movies and true stories are crazy.

I think it is crazy to see these miracle of life and still not believe.

That is CRAZY.

I do believe in JESUS.

I know a lot of people say why he has not come back to Earth.

I believe he has not come back because he did not sin.

Why would he ever want to come back to the world that does not believe in him?

The last time he was here man KILLED him.

I would not come back either.

Would you?

Last year I went pipelining I did not like the job.

I did not like living in camps.
To me it was almost like being in jail no freedom.
They tell you what you can or cannot do like they actually own you.

I never in my life have made that kind of money.
I was making about ten grand a month.
Great money but I was not a happy camper.

When I get released from camp.
I went home to my family.
They all thought I was happy because of the new job and the money.
Wrong I was happy and I mean happy because I was free.
So after spring break I did not go back to work.
I did not care about the money.
I LOVE myself enough to be happy.
My family all thought I was crazy for not to go back to work.
I am ok with that.
I think I was meant to be right here.
Right where I am in life.
Writing these words to you.

Chapter Six: Love

I have lots to talk about on this subject.
It has been proven that when we are in LOVE.
LOVE gives us a chemical reaction in our body's and mind giving a blissful feeling.
If we always gave unconditional LOVE and received unconditional LOVE I would think the chemical reaction in our bodies would give us incredible abilities.
Real mind blowing stuff.

Anita healed her own body.
How did she do that?
The doctors have no explanation with their limited ways of thinking.
If we have the power to heal ourselves what other abilities do we have if we only believed and truly learn to LOVE?
We are all here for a reason.
Maybe that reason is as simple as LOVE to LOVE and ENJOYS your life.
ENJOY all life.
Stop doing whatever does not make you happy and find your happiness.

I never even knew I had a dream until I started writing one week ago today.
Now I have 5624 words on paper.
I have never even written a shopping list.
Now I think I can write a book.
Proof it is never too late to have a dream.

When I was a youngster before the age of twelve.
I felt lots of LOVE from my family all kinds of LOVE.
At this time in my life I really could not say that my mom LOVES me more than my dad.
I remember how much fun I had as a child.
I really enjoyed my childhood.
AT the age of nine I met a young lady.

We went to the same school.
Over the years we became friends and I fell deeply in LOVE with (Heart Break 1).

I thought she was the most beautiful, smart exciting girl in the world.

When I was twelve years old I was lucky enough to be able to call (Heart Break 1) my girlfriend.

I was so happy life could not get any better.

At that time in my life I use to enjoy making people laugh.

I would write jokes down on slips of paper.
All the ones I thought to be funny.

My pockets were always full of deferent pieces of paper with jokes written on them.

One day I was walking around the school field with a friend.

I was going to tell him a joke.

I was going through my pockets to find the paper with the joke on it.
When I found a letter and I started to read it.

I did not have to finish reading it.

I got the message it was a dear john letter.
For the first time in my life my heart was crushed.

I know I was truly in LOVE because it was the kind of LOVE that I actually felt pain.

Our relationship was maybe one of the only relationships.
That did not end because of me being a dumbass.
Most of my relationships have ended because I can be the biggest dumbass of them all.

I was changed forever I never ever cared about having jokes in my pockets ever again.
It really took a long time for me to be able to laugh again I was so hurt.

I think that was the beginning of me pushing my parents away.
I started to rebel I did not care about anything.

I had lost all that mattered to me at that time in my life.

I never even considered letting the love from my parents that I have always felt heal me.

I just became very much closed off I lost all patience.

I would get mad over just about anything.

All I have ever wanted in life is to be LOVED and to LOVE.
It took a few years and a move before I would find LOVE again.

It is now four years later.

I am now sixteen years old.

I have my driver's license and I am feeling free.

My family and I move to a small town.

I hated the idea at the time.

I grew to LOVE our little town and the people there.
Within days of starting school I meet (Heart Break 2).
Life was once again beautiful for me.

This relationship lasted about six months.

I was not a very good boyfriend I was probably a little harsh.

We had our moments of what seemed like LOVE.

(Heart Break 2s) reason for breaking up with me.
Was that I had gotten kicked out of school and that was not going to work for her.
YA it must have been true love.

That was sarcasm. Lol.

I once again had my Heart removed from my chest.

I was heartbroken but to be honest I did not feel physical pain like the first heart break.
Only two months of my life to pass by this time before I was willing to give LOVE another try.

This time I met a beautiful lady.

"Beauty" was a year older than me and it took no time at all to become great friends.

We really had no commitments to each other.

We just were.

"Beauty" was my first real sexual experience.

I found her to be so beautiful.
Just a true blessing such a beautiful person.
I think I will get to meet her in all my lives.
There were adult reasons why "Beauty" and I stopped seeing each other.
We never stopped being friends.
As easily as we got together it was over.
"Beauty" never made me any promises and she never broke my heart.
I will always LOVE her.
To this day I think about her and hold her in my heart every day.
I LOVE you.
Thanks for being a friend.

Another year of my life passes me by.
I remember being very lonely.
I wanted a relationship so bad.

I again met a young lady (Heart Break 3).
This relationship was totally my fault for not working.

I was doing a lot of partying and experimenting with drugs and alcohol.

I truly do believe I LOVED, (Heart Break 3).
We were together for about two years on and off.
I believe (Heart Break 3) LOVED me but over the couple of years that we spent together.
I wore her down and ruined the LOVE she had for me.
I would go out drinking and cheat if given the chance.

This is the relationship that gives me the suicide story that you read a few chapters back.
I probably took more life lessons from this relationship than any other.

The end of this relationship once again crushed me but I learnt what happens when you cheat?

You lose the one you truly LOVE for a few moments of passion. When if I was smart I could have had more passion with the one I LOVE.

I literally thought to myself as I always do.

I knew this was all my fault and I swore to myself I would never think that little about the person I claim to LOVE by cheating ever again and I never have.

We stayed in contact over the years until she passed away because of an illness.
In I am thinking 2001.

I am truly sorry for not knowing what the date was of her death.
I am close on the year.

(Heart Break 3) knows that I had to do everything that I have done with my life to get me right here.
Right to this point in life.

Many years of my LIFE blow by.

I say blow by because I think any year spent thinking you are not LOVED is a waste of our life.

If we think about it LOVE is not sex.
Yes sex is better when done with the one you love.

I love sex but we all know.
Sex can be ENJOYED with or without LOVE being involved.

I think it is just way better with LOVE.

I think I would confuse sex and love.

I guess if we LOVED unconditional.

LOVE would be involved in everything we do.

So what I am trying to get at before I started thinking about sex and got lost is we always having LOVE in our life.

We cannot see it but if we let ourselves we could maybe feel LOVE.

We would never feel loss if we truly LOVED.

We would understand things were just not meant to be.

Rather than wasting life on feeling heart broke.

I am an expert in wasting life trust me.

My heart has been broke way more times than I am going to write about in this book.

That could be a book all on its own.

I started stuccoing in 1988 in White Rock B.C.

One of my all-time favorite places.

Just Beautiful.

I fell in love with the job.

So a couple of years go by I make the move to Courtney B.C. another very beautiful place.

I did a bit of mountain biking on the Island.

I have seen a lot of real beauty all over the Island.

I love Courtney B.C. so much that I thought if I am ever lucky enough to ever have a son.

I wanted to name him "Courtney James."

I never had that kind of luck.

I have learned that is OK.

Everything is always going to be OK.

I do not think we should live places we do not find beautiful.

How could we be happy?

I spend a couple years on the island

And meet a young lady and fall in LOVE with (Heart Break 4).

I again ruined this relationship.

I have never hit any lady my weapon of choice has always been my mouth.

I do not know why but sometimes I can say the harshest things.

I want the words to hurt I guess.

I am working on that problem.

Thanks to Anita and her story.

I now know I have been living in fear.

NOT ANY MORE.

I think maybe I was scared of being alone and many other things.
So I take my broken heart and leave the island.

I move back home it is a small town with not too much work for me.
So I move back to the town I grew up in.
Where my heart was first crushed.

Stucco is a hard job to make a lot of money at because it is seasonal.
Down south you can at least work a full year.
I enjoy spreading mud enough that I struggle through it.
I Just collect E.I. in the winter that barely gets me by.

When I was at my parents house.
I met a young lady and her daughter.
We moved in together and we tried to become a family.
We spent a couple of hard years together.
We defiantly never had any extra money.

Near the end of our relationship.
We were not getting along so we decided to go our separate ways.
We just did not work well together.
Both of our lives took off for the better when we separated.

We also never stopped being friends until her very tragic accident in 2008.
She passed away from a house fire.
The smoke got to her.
Way before this very tragic accident happened.
We separated in April of 1997.

I started hydro blasting a very dangerous job with good pay and benefits.
I was feeling pretty good about life.
On one Saturday in May my sister and brother in law came over to visit me.

My niece and nephew were playing out back and we were in side.

We decided I should go for a bottle of rye.
When I am in the liquor store I see a vision of BEAUTY.

I am usually pretty shy when it comes to women but for some reason I was not shy on this day in May.

I thought I should ask
(BEAUTIFUL) if she wants to come over for a drink.

She said no so I thought ya ok.
Then we were at the checkout at the same time.
So I asked her again (BEAUTIFUL) said no once again.
Now I am starting to get self-conscious.

Then on our way out the door I held the door open for her.
Once again I ask (BEAUTIFUL) and explain to her.
That there are children running around outside at my place.
It would be a safe place to be.

I asked (BEAUTIFUL) to follow me home so that she could go pick up her friend and come back if she wanted.

I was hoping that made her feel safer.

(BEAUTIFUL) said yes.

I was kind of shocked.

She followed me home.
When we got to my place (BEAUTIFUL) came in and we had a visit.
After a few hours of hanging out and talking.

(BEAUTIFUL) asked if "I wanted to go to her friend's party."
Of course I said yes.

I believe my last relationship had to be bad and recent.
So that I would appreciate how good my relationship was with (BEAUTIFUL.)

I did know it was special even at the time.
If we were mad at each other.

We just did not talk until she forgave me.
Ha-ha.

I was not use to that at all being angry and not fighting.

I did enjoy it.
It sure made it easier to make up.

If we were not at work we were together every day from the first day I met her.

(BEAUTIFUL) was my best friend.

I usually would wake up and watch her sleep.

I can remember one morning I woke up before her.
The sun was shining in through our bedroom window.

She looked so BEAUTIFUL a picture perfect moment.

I can remember thinking how much I never wanted that moment to end.
So I took a picture.
A BEAUTIFUL picture.

I do not have the picture anymore but I do not even have to shut my eyes to see that moment in time.

I can picture her right now not in a crazy way honestly.
When I think of her I can picture her in my mind without having to close my eyes.
Do you understand me?

I hope so.

In 1999 I started getting these uneasy feelings.

I thought my job being dangerous was going to kill me and take me away from (BEAUTIFUL).

I had such strong feeling about this so I quit my job and went back to stucco.

On Friday September the 17th 1999.

I was working in Fort ST. James B.C. with my boss and his twenty-year-old son.
On our way home I had the door seat.

My boss was driving and his son was in the middle of the seat.

I was sleeping when across the radio comes the words
"A young woman died at xxxx mill today."

I woke up in tears.
Somehow I heard exactly what was said on the radio.

I knew in my heart the guy on the radio was talking about (BEAUTIFUL).

My boss also new (BEAUTIFUL).
He was friends with her mom and dad.
We had stucco their house a couple of years before I met (BEAUTIFUL).
That was the first time I saw her).
At that time I just did my job.

I never talked to her she was way to young then only a teenager.
My boss tried to comfort me by telling me there is other lady's that work at the mill.
I knew he was right about there being other lady's working there.
I knew in my heart (BEAUTIFUL) was gone.
I mean the tears were gushing no way I could stop.

Then his cell rings and I hear him say, "He's sitting right here" and hands me the phone.
It was his wife.
She tried to tell me what happened and I cut her off from talking.
I told her "I know."
That was about all I could get out through the tears.
She asked, "how do you know?"
I replied back, "I know" and pass the cell back to my boss.

That turned out to be the longest hour drive of my life.
It was almost like time slowed down for me.
Life kind of stopped for me on that day.
I have done a lot of thinking and wishing since September 17 1999.
I do not believe I have been living since that day.
I have been going through the motions of life but in no way have I been living.

It is now seventeen years later and I still think about (BEAUTIFUL) every day.

I still LOVE her to this day and beyond.

Here are some numbers I thought about.

(BEAUTIFUL) was 23 when she passed away I was 32.

She was born in 76 I was born in 67.

The numbers are the same just backward.

I know it does not mean anything.

These are just some of the thoughts I had.

I was trying to find a reason for such a loss.

Doing the usual.

Why me how could this happen to me?

I was being selfish I never lost my LIFE.

I sure was acting like I lost my life.

I should have just been thinking of (BEAUTIFUL'S) life.

I would have been much happier.

I put you through having to read my depressing LOVE life to make a point.

I had to live through all that.

Now you have to.

The point I am trying to make is I still believe in LOVE.

All the loss and what seems like a never-ending quest for LOVE.

I still believe in LOVE.

Now after seeing Anita's story.

I now know the key to life is to LOVE and to LOVE LIFE.

ENJOY LIFE.

I have become a hermit.

Closed myself off from the world.

I am going to listen to Anita and

LOVE myself my LIFE and of course all of you.

I am going to enjoy all the beauty in the world.

I know some of my views have changed from the beginning of this book.

That is because of Anita's story.

I just learned about her like I said.
So yes one or two of my thoughts and views have changed.
After all she's been there.

She would know way more than me.
She confirmed my beliefs in an afterlife.

I am not too sure what happened on march fifth but for
whatever reason I started writing.

I LOVE writing I LOVE my life.

I am going to try real hard to LOVE more.
Well I am going to try and learn how to LOVE more.

RANDOM THOUGHTS

Most of what I have written down here is all random thoughts.
That is why I am writing it so fast.
Some of what I have wrote.
I have given serious thought to over the years.
Like reincarnation, death and LOVE.

Back to random.
I was thinking we should start a community.
That lives off of LOVE and NATURE. Then it came to me.
Is that how the Amish live.
I am not too sure but I think they try to live LIFE pure.
By this I mean without technologies.
They ride horses.
No cars.
I would LOVE the freedom of being able to go out to my horse
and head out for a beautiful nature ride.
Would not need to worry about fuel or any of modern man's
limitations.
Just ride and be free.

I think maybe when it comes to fortune tellers.
This is just my view and thoughts on it.
No offense I really have no proof.

I am thinking maybe by what Anita said, She could see her
present life and previous life's all happening at once.

She does not mention a future LIFE.
So I am thinking.
The future really has not happened yet for anybody.
Where she was life on earth was still rolling by all at once.
With earth moving forward always being consent.

So I am thinking GOD does not know what is coming because it
has not happened yet.
I do not believe anybody can tell what has not happened yet.
We defiantly should learn from our past to make for a better

future.

If we had passed lives like Anita said.
It only stands to reason we are going to have a future life.
Why not try and make a better life.

A better future for us all.

If we believed we are coming back which I do.

We would treat our planet better.

So many times I have heard and I might even have said this.
When I was young and dumb.
"I do not care by then I will be long gone."
Wrong we are all going to be living in the garbage we leave
ourselves.

Time to start thinking of the future of our home our planet.

We need to make a happier tomorrow.

Maybe not knowing the future is the beauty of life.

We are always learning.

I do like the idea of making my own future.
So I do not believe it would be possible to ever create a time
machine that goes forward into the future.
Nothing has happened yet.

I do believe we could go back in time.

The past is all we can know.

The future is a blank slate.
One thing for sure the future is for all of us and we are the only ones
that can make it a better future.

Knowing I will see my LOVED ones again in Heaven.
Knowing the unconditional LOVE that waits for me.
Knowing all this.
To tell you the truth makes me excited for death.

I do not think we should think of ourselves as being on top of
the food chain.

We are above the food chain.
We do know there is such a thing as the food chain.
We can keep ourselves from being eaten. loll
So I think we are above the food chain.
We are not on the same level as the creatures of Earth.
We are above them.

We should start thinking of ourselves as being GODS.
Not being vain or evil GODS.
Being KIND, GENTLE, CARING and LOVING GODS.
Can you imagine the world we would live in.?
At the very least we should think of ourselves as the GODS that create our own futures.

<u>Chapter Seven: Life</u>

I believe women should be treated higher than the man.
Woman give life men take life.
I would think the power to give birth to create life.
That to me is a GODDESS.
Being a man I know the only thing I can do is LOVE.
I cannot give birth I can go halves but that is it.
I can give the GODESS my offering.
She alone has the body to create LIFE out of our offering.
Again just my thoughts.

I am sorry to offend all the silly men out there.
That think they somehow are better or more special.
Then the only thing on earth that gives life.
Your moms and her fellow females.
Thank GOD for all of you.

Maybe the old native ways are the right ways to live.
Where the men hunt and the women stay at camp.
That is not because a woman cannot hunt.
It is because she does not have to.
She already does enough.
Women are the key to a future.
Without women there is no future.
So in saying that.
I think women should not have to work.
You can do whatever makes you happy.
I am sorry that it sounds like I am telling you what you can do.
I am just telling you I agree with what you already know.

Ok I just had a thought.
Many of you will not agree with me.
Trust me I am jealous and that has probably been why most of my
relationships did not work.

If we LOVE ourselves and others unconditionally.
Like Anita says that is the key to life.
Knowing this we would not get jealous.
So would that create a world where we have random sex?
With anybody because we all LOVE equally.
Or would that make a world that had more trust more LOVE?

I am guessing we would LOVE our soul mate so much.
That we would never have the desire to cheat.

I think the only fear worth having. Should be the fear of hurting
you mate or really hurting anybody.
I am thinking having that fear could make us better human
beings.
It would have too.
If we all had that fear the most in life.
Not the fear of death or being scared of not being loved or accepted.
The fear of hurting all you LOVE.

The only by product of a world like this would be.
LOVE and KINDESS for all.

I think if you do not agree with me on this or anything I say.
That is OK.
Everything is always going to be ok.

I do not see why or how we let people that play a game all their
lives.
A team sport.
Get paid such an outrages amount of money.
Any team sport should pay a more believable wage.
Maybe like the average person.
They also should receive free medical for life.
If you athletes do not like that go get a real job.
Ticket sales would come down in prices.
If GOD blessed you to be faster and stronger than your team mates
cool you will get all the lady's and maybe be someone's hero.
In no way are you working any harder than your team mates.

The teammates that take that check so you can score or get in a fight to protect you.
All teammates should get an equal wage.

No way should a star or sports hero.
Get paid more than a fireman or policeman.
They give their lives for us on a daily basis.
Could you imagine the police force we would have?
If they got paid for the service they provide?

If they get shot and live.
That should be like winning the lottery for them.
They should get to go and enjoy the rest of their lives.

I cannot believe we live in a world. Where the harder you work the less pay you get.
The less you do the more pay you get.
This just seems so wrong to me.
There is no reason for this.

We all need to grab a grip.
Why do we not stop the need to be better or think that we are better than the person working beside us?

No one with money.
Is better than a person without money.
We are all EQUALS.
We all have something positive to offer the world.
That is why we are all here.

Anita said in the other realm.
She felt like we were all one.
I am thinking maybe we need to get back to that way of living.
We should act like we are all one right here right now.
We should all think about ways to make the world a better place and act on them.
If it is actually going to improve all our lives.
It must be right.

If we cannot become a world of equals.
Then I think this is the only right way of doing things.
The people that work the hardest should be the highest paid.
That would give us all incentive to work harder.
The more you know the more you get paid.
This would give us all incentive for knowledge.

Of course our country is broke.
Our leaders send our tax money to other countries.
We spend all our money buying products made from other countries.
If we keep our tax money in our own country.
Buy products from our own country.
We might not be broke.

The tax money that is collected would be able to maintain our roads.
I hit a pothole that was so bad it took both front and back tires out.
So I asked a cop.
If I could go to the city and get them to pay for my tires.
He told me that it was a privilege to drive on our roads.
Well if that was true.
Then why do we pay road taxes when we buy gas.
We live in such a corrupt world.

I do not have any children.
That might be why this makes me so mad.
I can only think of the evil that has to be clouding our judgment.
As a parent you would never hand your child a pack of smokes.
So why do you let them play with a cell phone.
They are a radiation device that is stuck to your child's ear.
It is proven that cell phones cause brain cancer in children.
Do not believe me look it up.

I will tell you why you chose to play the percent game with your children's brain.

It is because you are a lazy parent.
Instead of taking time out of your day to teach and play with your child.

You plop them in front of a T.V. or give them a gadget that is known to cause brain cancer.
To do the parenting for you.

I sure hope we do not end up with a generation of CHILDREN with brain cancer.
All because of being a lazy parent.

What is going to happen if your child comes down with brain cancer.
The first thing that is coming out of your mouth is "GOD why me why my child how can you do this to us?"
Guess what?
Do not blame GOD.
GOD did not give your child the RADIATION device.
You did.

We all have to start taking responsibility for our actions or lack of action.
By realizing you your self-caused this not GOD.
Time to wake up people.

As I said about women.
We have no future without children.
Time to save our children and make sure we all have a future.
I am not sorry for hurting anybody's feelings on this matter.
Wake up spend time with your children before it is too late.
GOD sees everything.
WAKE UP.

RANDOM THOUGHTS

Again I want to say sorry if some of my thoughts are contradictive.
This is caused by my random thoughts.
If I am thinking about something.
     I am coming up with both sides of an argument.
Only on matters I have given a lot of thought to.

    Sorry that some chapters are so short.
That is because I do not have much experience in that topic.
     I have never given it much thought until now.
     I still have an opinion.
     I am not telling anybody how to live.
    You are all given the freedom of thought and WILL.
     I just think it is time for us to start thinking.
Thinking about our future.

     I am living in the comfort that I know where I am going when I
leave this body.
With the body I leave behind.
Chuck it in the ocean tie a weight to it and feed some fish.
     I do not care I am done with it.
Might as well do some kind of good and feed one of GODS creations
with it.

    This is something I have never thought about.
     Anita said when she was in the other realm.
"We leave behind our bodies and our sex (male, female).

    So there is a good chance that I have been a woman before and
got to
Experience the joy of motherhood.
     I really do not think so but I will keep an open mind.

     I think that if I am keeping my thoughts when I cross over and
if we are all one in Heaven.
     I am thinking I have always been male when I come to Earth.
     I think for the reason of always being one sex on Earth.
That would explain homosexuality.

The truth behind the idea that they were meant to be the opposite sex.
I am thinking they are exactly right.

Have you ever heard of life going full circle?
I am thinking that is a reality.
The full circle of life is birth, death and back to birth over and over again.
Evolution.

I am thinking that bits and pieces of all religious beliefs are true.
Maybe one or two views from all religions are right.

Maybe GODS idea with placing life all over the world.
GOD knew we would seek answers. So we would go out in search of knowledge but instead of learning from each other.
We kill each other.

I am thinking if we can take all the beliefs in the world and put them together.
We probably could come up with some answers we need.
If we compared and took the most common beliefs we might be on to something.

I do not claim to know any religion.
I just do not believe in them.
Whatever makes you happy.

I do not think I really care about why we are here anymore I am just glad we are.

I think if there is a devil.
That is the force that keeps people wanting oil and needing to cut down trees.

Drilling into our planet and then with drawing oil is so retarded in my way of thinking.

Why would we ever drill into our own planet.

If you have the need to drill go and drill on a planet I do not want a future on please.

When we can produce oil and fuel without drilling.

This is proven we can.

Why do we continue to drill?

No need to drill.

I do not get it.

That to me is either retarded or evil.

How do we know what oil is in the earth for?

Maybe it causes the energy that makes our rotation?

I am thinking if we keep draining the oil.

What if we cause the rotation to stop or become lopsided by draining all the oil from one side of the planet.

I do not know but I really do not want to find out.

Do you.

Stop the evil that is money.

Logging is the other evil.

Why would we cut off our air supply?

Again retarded.

Anything that is made by trees.

Can be made from a crop that only takes months to grow not hundreds of years.

Has to be an evil force.

I do not want to put down anybody that works and supports their families from these jobs.

There still would be jobs you would just be using a different product.

A product that can stop the drilling into our planet and stop the raping and pillaging that is going on with our air supply.

Car companies have almost cut out all human workers out.

I think they should have to slow production down.

They should only be allowed to make a limited amount of new cars.

They could use their other time in a year just developing new and better parts.

I am not telling you what to spend your money on.
If it makes you happy to buy a new car or truck then go for it.

My car is now paid for.

I LOVE my car it has been a part of my life now for eight years.

So I am going to take the $500 a month payment.
That turns into $6000, a year.

I am taking that $6000 and every year put it into my car.

I am going to make it the car I want.

I do LOVE my car but I would trade it for a horse in a second.

I think we have to start realizing that what makes me happy may not make you happy.
So stop trying to tell me what I can do or cannot do.

I am going to do what makes me happy.
It is my LIFE.

I am not telling anyone how to live.
Do what makes you happy.

I am only giving my thoughts.
Agree with me or not.

I am going to be happy earthier way.
If you really want to know what makes someone happy ask them do not tell them.

I can guarantee I would never give up LOVE for money.

I would pick sleeping beside a park bench if my LOVE was sleeping on the bench.
Over being rich and alone any day.

I in no means have been living proper.

I use to hate and judge.

I am going to let my heart grow and hopefully I will LOVE and try to understand people.

Rather than hate and judge.

I do not want to hurt anybody's feelings these are only my thoughts.

Agree or don't.

 All up to you.

I want to thank Anita for sharing her beautiful story and confirming my beliefs in an afterlife.

I want to thank my parents for the LOVE they have always shown me even when they do not agree with me.

I LOVE you.

THANKS.

Thanks to all of you.

I hope you enjoyed my Story's.

I hope I gave some of you some new thoughts and confirmed some of the stuff you already know.

So be KIND and share your LOVE.

I am going to leave you for now with this thought.

(There is never an END; only beautiful new beginnings)

Keith McDougall
30/03/2016

Manufactured by Amazon.ca
Acheson, AB